Courtney Love has gone on record calling losing the role of Satine to Nicole Kidman [in Moulin Rouge] 'one of the biggest disappoints' of her career and made no secret of her resentment against Kidman.

Director Baz Luhrmann characterized the difference between the two actresses in a Vanity Fair article by saying "Courtney is fire and Nicole is ice."

"It's no secret me and Kidman don't like each other."

On Letterman, Love quoted a Vanity Fair magazine article calling the two actresses "fire and ice", saying she had put down the Cold Mountain star when they were both in a lift together by telling Nicole:
"That means you're a puddle."

—Anonymous, fuckyeahcourtneylove.com

'The work of art is a letter addressed if at all to strangers, if need be from other galaxies. Art itself is perhaps humanity's last domain, the final autonomy, at its best DISTURBANCE. But the era of letters and diaries as a means of expressing feeling/idea/pain has ended with the dawn of the electronic age. Communication by machines, with which the process of creation, and with it the chance of error, has been dissolved in a concoction of deafening precision and lightning speed. The ice age of no dialogue between minds, hearts, spirits has begun, the only escape route leads down, into dreams, for some, into the cemetery.' (Theatremachine, Heiner Müller)

My friend Sarah told me there was something retro about my *Phone Plays*, because talking on the phone as a general form of social life has dramatically decreased in recent generations. Many people consider it rude and alarming to be called on the phone, out of the blue or at all. I'm sadly one of those people. A sense of dread usually sets in when my phone rings, and I find spending time in two places at once, with a disembodied voice and my own suddenly-emerging phone persona (also somewhat disembodied—projected into an unknown, real and imagined room) to be pretty uncomfortable. But we'll always talk on the phone, right? In emergencies at the very least. But every phone call *acts* like an emergency. It starts with an alarm (whether it rings or vibrates, it produces a sound), like honking a car horn. It's a form of communication reduced to an essential urgent demand for attention (and in the case of the horn, discipline), which one is free to attempt to ignore, but not from its innate imposition / insertion. Like a child crying.

Its urgent affect is also its theatricality—it takes place in the present, even when it's in the past. But its general style is also theatrical—a style of desperation, its noise—the term "melodrama" originates from a combination of the Greek *melos*, meaning "melody" or "song" and the French word *drame*, meaning "drama."

The phone call is a genre of communication that takes place in the *almost present*. If the technology is working appropriately, the implicit delay required by the technology's transferral is sublimated; like all technology, it supports whilst also distorting, alienating users from their initial utterance (if we weren't already alienated from it), whilst also threatening to break, malfunction, leaving its users alone again.

Here's Matilda Bernstein Sycamore from *The Freezer Door*:

The quality of my life has significantly declined since the social norm of talking on the phone to friends shifted from a common assumption to a rare commodity. I can't help thinking this is just another way of giving into distance. How people act like their fear of talking on the phone is something so unique and they don't know why, but actually it's a dominant cultural norm. Or people embrace the norm, and act offended when you question it. It makes sense to me that people who grew up texting might be skittish about talking on the phone, but then there are people older than me who will say they've always been afraid. And maybe that's true. I just wish people had stopped talking on the phone in order to see one another more often, but unfortunately it's just to never see one another.'

Heiner Müller's and Elfriede Jelinek's plays are an object and an obstacle that are handed over to the director and the actor, stoking the tension and conflict between text and performance. *'Theater is a series of synaptic intersections that occur between the actors and their characters, their props, the words they're speaking and their gestures [...]. Even though the plays rehearsed and circumscribed, the act of theater really happens in the tiny gaps between actors and their roles, a friction witnessed by the audience.'* (*Aliens and Anorexia*, Chris Kraus)

I'm an artist and a writer, so ideally each play will have some consequence in art and literature, but that's not up to me. The plays in this collection have a lot in common with (and could be read aloud as) closet dramas—a literary form popular in the 18th century, a play written to be read aloud by one performer and therefore implying less practical barriers to its distribution, often written by women, who were usually financially and politically excluded from the theatre. This form interests me because the economic pressure is right there, implicitly, and I started writing after art school because:

1. Sustaining an art practice seemed practically and financially impossible in London.
2. Writing is (sort of) free.

I wrote myself back to art with my first book *People Person*: a novella following an art school drop-out discovering the things he does when he black-out drinks through conversations with 'friends.' The jump from there to where I am now has been through the question of the 'real' in a text. The reality of the contemporary art world felt like too big of a distraction from making discrete art objects to circulate in its economy. Art says one thing and does another. I wanted to be honest.

When I edit my writing, I always read it aloud. It is the only way I can tell if a piece is working, by hearing it in space, not silently, neurotically inside my head—'my characters live only insofar as they speak,' (*Women in German Yearbook: Feminist Studies in German Literature & Culture*, University of Nebraska Press, Elfriede Jelinek)—and I think that's true of real people too, or I want it to be true. Expression in space is the only real expression, according to Artaud.

Consequently, I am always returning to this moment of extension, of loss and gain, the possibility of affirming/exiting/exploding one body and inserting into another. The sculptor and painter Cathy Wilkes meditates on the moment Jochebed pushes a basket containing her child away, as the Nile's own muscular currents pull it from her. I am concerned with the capacity and possibility of speaking to a 'real' world—'out there'—that we all take part in. Often I think being fake, unnatural, deceitful, insincere, and inauthentic is the closest one can get to the real and the honest— *'Use artifice to strip artifice of artifice.'* (Carl Dreyer, from Eileen Myles' introduction to *I Love Dick*, Chris Kraus)

'I'm fake, but I'm real-fake' is something I say when I'm drinking and getting to know someone, because I can tell that most people think I am overperforming, to the point of becoming disingenuous. I want those people to know that I know what I'm doing, I just can't stop, and I usually don't want to.

'Theatre has the task of asserting that vitality against the pressure and/ or demand merely to reproduce reality. For it is at this point that theatre threatens reality, and this is surely its most political function[...] if art does not threaten reality, then it has no function and it is nonsense to spend money on it.' (*Theatremachine*, Heiner Müller)

The onus for the *Phone Plays* project began when I was walking across the bridge towards the National Theatre. Unsubtle, pedestrian, rolling text that reveals itself letter by letter is installed on the surface of the building. The building speaks clearly but slipperily, visible but ungraspable, which appeals to me—the possibility of speaking directly to an audience with little room for misunderstanding and yet without a resolute opportunity to comprehend—revealing some essential inalienable truth about communication: I could try and try to speak to you, and never be understood. Or inversely, I could make no sense at all, completely baffle your everyday understanding of language's grammar, its rules, and still resonate with you intensely—you might know exactly where I'm coming from. You might feel extremely close to me, you might say *'I understand you.'*

'Communication Technology has increased communication and decreased understanding.' (What's Love (or Care, Intimacy, Warmth, Affection) Got to Do with It?, Paul Chan)

I read this quote after writing two of these plays, and it made sense to me. I would say that my characters take part in this contemporary flow of desire; they communicate without understanding; but the texts themselves, which moved between theatre and poetry contexts as I wrote them, at times could produce understanding without communication—some pre-verbal resonance perhaps. Rhythm and tone are important, but they're somewhat out of my hands in these works. It's a relief. That's something extremely rewarding about the theatre, or specifically in being a playwright—it lets you dissociate, be present and absent, someone uses your body and you (usually more intensely) use someone else's body (the actor's). All you can do is try to communicate clearly and transparently about your desires, listen to your collaborators' desires, and hope that this experience is rewarding for everyone involved, because taking the risk seems worth it.

Some other quotes I think of often are:

'His writing isn't about something, it is something.'

(Our Exagmination Round the Factification for Incamination of Work in Progress (1929), Samuel Beckett referring to Joyce's *Ulysses*. Still the best compliment that could be given to an artwork or piece of writing in my eyes)

and

'If I surround an area with a fence or a line or otherwise, the purpose may be to prevent someone from getting in or out; but it may also be part of a game and the players supposed, say, to jump over the boundary.' (*Philosophical Investigations*, Wittgenstein)

These are quotes I always give to artists and writers, and both have informed the methodology of my practice practically and thoughtfully. These ideas have led me to ask myself: How can I insist on paying attention to my desire (even as it reifies and reproduces familiar or imperfect objects), not as an inherent lack, but as a momentum in the world (what Deleuze and Guattari might call 'desiring-production') in which I take part? 'Desire makes us do things,' and I want to think about these things but even more than that, I want to *do* things. I want to go through compelling, implicit, seemingly inescapable images into something else, something surprising (the theatre should always surprise you). But to do that, I can't turn off my body, I can't ignore my desire, and I won't. *'Alas, the problem with desire is 'we rarely want the things we should.'* (*Females*, Andrea Long Chu, quoted in *The Right To Sex*)

In *Blanks* the audience becomes an object, put into the role of the comatose partner (we assume) of an anonymous woman. She can't hear us, we can't reach her: the form of the phone call, with its economy of means, teases out a sort of science fiction scenario whereby the innate alienation, extraction and projection of the body is brought to the surface of a theatrical experience, through the pulpy, soapy gimmick of the comatose lover.

Plague was my reaction to this first step. I wanted to write a character within the phone call genre who was closer to the 'real' world tension of talking on the phone with a stranger—*being contacted*—being forced out of your life and into someone else's. Having your life and your body changed, it happens all day—*'you cannot consent to yourself.'* (*Females*, Andrea Long Chu)

I wrote a play about a social worker and incorporated the real aesthetic touches used by this professionalised care procedure/realm. To my disappointment, it was boring, as phone calls usually are, and I wasn't a performance artist invested in pushing for some 'natural' experience of the 'real,' I was a playwright, interested in the thrilling and perverse capacities of the 'theatre and its double,' (the real). (*The Theatre and its Double*, Antonin Artaud)

I decided to do the opposite of what I had done. Instead of being caring and attempting to repair the social world professionally, and performing her job appropriately, she destroys it. She is ambivalent to the point of being self-centred and cruel. I was interested in the kind of labour being performed here. When the character expresses herself, confesses her true feelings, she is not only being an insensitive and unkind person, she is also sabotaging a flow of production. That's the thing about the care industry, it's an industry. The script itself is informed by the formal constraints that a piece of theatre on the phone affords, and how the history of the theatre is partly concerned with figuring out how to make something visible/communicable/compelling/attention-holding. I was thinking about how Greek tragedies were performed in huge stadiums to large audiences, something closer to competitive sport than the classical and historical mode in which they're presented today. And so the stories that emerge and live on are amplified, crystallised appeals to 'essential' fears/anxieties/desires, greatly informed by their contexts and technologies. Some people believe the reason for a recent influx in incest porn narratives is because of its ability to appeal to its prospective audiences desire with a very reduced means of communication. Reading 'DAD FUCKS SON' on an advertisement within the sidebar of the porn website you are watching porn on leaves little room for misunderstanding, and arouses a potential narrative pull simply through its economically expressed power dynamic. Between the speaker and the distributor there is a conflict.

What does the genre of the phone call afford us? What are we all saying to each other when we talk on the phone whilst all saying something else? What are the objects in our hands saying? What is the voice saying? This object of the body, its sound, removed from its body, does it haunt you? These disembodied voices, do they elicit panic? Sensuality? Anxiety? Ambivalence?

'It is essential to put an end to the subjugation of the theatre to the text, and to recover the notion of a kind of unique language halfway between gesture and thought,' (The Theatre and its Double, Antonin Artaud). Theatre is the place where thought finds its body, but in these plays, the protagonists find then lose their bodies once again. They give it away, have it taken, claw it back. Speech is expressed and extracted from these characters. There's a tension in these works between the body and the economic/technical constraints it expresses itself with/against/through. When a body becomes just a voice, we experience it in a way that brings it close to thought again.

These plays were motivated by a desire to make theatre with limited resources. There aren't a lot of options for playwrights to have their work performed, and coming from a fine art background, I can't say I know what those options are. I first performed this project at the Tom of Finland fair in London where I was also working as a receptionist. I was invited by Ridley Road Project Space and it felt like a success based on the feedback from my friends and the actor I collaborated with—but I couldn't really know. No matter how much a playwright writes or a director directs, 'the actor on stage has the final say,' (*Theatre For Beginners*, Richard Maxwell). This process intensified that logic, alienating me completely from its performance. I found this pleasurable and sustainable—a way to do theatre relatively cheaply and independently, plus, much of the anxiety was removed from the equation. The work itself was a secret shared between an actor and an audience member. I was happily excluded from it.

So I kept doing them—presenting my second phone play at my first rundgang at Städelschule in Frankfurt. Hardly anyone heard it or even saw it—multiple audience members walked right through it believing it not to be an artwork at all. A few people encouraged me to make it 'visible' by placing it on a plinth, but I knew its invisibility was the work's strength; the fact that it could be performed anywhere, with minimal preparation—all that was needed was an actor, a phone, a sim card, and a place to charge it.

I knew that the work had a disturbing and perverse potential—like Hamad Butt's *Cradle*, an installation consisting of glass baubles containing lethal levels of chlorine gas, suspended from the ceiling, threatening his audience. Something that interests me is this idea that anyone in the world could contact you at any time and say the most devastating, appalling thing to you. iPhones are flat, tight objects with a capacity that exceeds their immediate form, collapsing time and space if the actor wanted to, if I could figure out a good line. 'A good line sounds true.' (*Mad Pepper*, Eileen Myles)

Blanks and *Plague* might be melodramas. It's hard to define but one of the genre's calling cards is passive men and active women, something both these plays have. The next two plays I wrote were a departure from this, an attempt to surprise myself, push the form further and incorporate what I'd learnt from previous performances. Each time a play was installed in an art space the phone's implicit reservation would quickly become too much, almost camp, before returning to their inert and alienated general condition. But when the work was done in a theatre, the painfulness and awkwardness of the works were brought forth, as theatre audiences were more accustomed to submitting to duration and the rules/regimes of attention. They resented sitting still with the work—but they needn't have had to. It was after this experience that I wrote *Central Auto*, sat in a car driving back to England for Christmas. I had seen how combative my works could be, and I wanted to find a way to incorporate the audience more whilst still submitting them to my text—I want to write plays, not performances.

It was embarrassing and awkward when I started writing plays, I think. I don't know, I don't really remember, even though it wasn't that long ago. I think the moment I started writing for the theatre was simply the moment I started reading my writing aloud. I know beginning my novella was seriously excruciating, but once you're in the habit the pain comes and goes, you get used to it. Something I know for sure is that you can't do the theatre alone. I never would have written and performed a play if my friend Edward hadn't shown me how to, and my friend George hadn't told me to. Someone once said to me art is capitalism and the theatre is socialism. It's not true, but it sounds true.

In this play, the speaker cannot always hear the audience at the other end of the phone. Maybe sometimes she hears something, she barely makes it out, she wonders—*did I imagine it?* Her attention shifts, she is distracted from finishing what she was saying. This rhythm of stopping, hearing her audience—opening up an awkward invisible stage for her audience—this rhythm belongs to *her* (the actor). She responds to her live audience, yes, but the actor may also deploy this rhythm without a cue from her audience. It's up to her. The rhythm is hers.

Characters:

VOICE.   Her voice has the texture of a gifted recording artist, not a gifted singer. *She knows the texture of her voice.*
NURSE.   On stage only briefly, she's working.

Author's Notes:

...   This at the start or end of a sentence indicates a trailing in or off of a sentence, some distance

VOICE.   Hello
Can you hear me?
I'm here
(Sighing, whispering.) Of course of course of course
I'm here
The traffic was—and I'm sorry you had to be on your own
You can forgive me
...You aren't alone now
Listen to me going on
If you could find a way to
To speak to me

...

Or show me
Somehow

...

Let me know you can hear me
That you're in there

...

Don't hurt yourself
I'm not threatening you I'm not mad at you
(To NURSE.*)* What should I say to him?
*(*NURSE *leaves.)*
You have to rest, but
I miss you
And the doctors are saying...
Don't worry about what the doctors are saying, listen to me

...

It's me
Can you feel that?
It's my hand
And my ring
My hands touching your hand
Is it cold?
I'm here, see?
...I want.... to say... I can feel you
That I can sense you
And I can
Yes you can hear me
I know it

...

You have a vein on your head,
You're not *quite* relaxed
You're still a person

I'm touching it
Softly
It's soft, it's like a...
piece of air
It looks like...
Well
It looks like a...
Or you look like a...
I suppose
Haha
I hope you're laughing in there
I hope that that's.... ok...?
I could touch you like that
Like your whole body was... a...
Would you like that?
Like you're...
...Trapped in a...
You used to like that
When I...
Uh...
Haha

...

The nurse has gone it's just me

...

When I...
Undressed
You
...Like a...
...Like you were for...
And you just lay there
Taking it all in
Watching me
I could do it again
...I should stop
For God's sake look at where you are
...Although
Have you ever? In a hospital?

...

I have ... actually
...Sorry I know you get jealous I won't say any more
Unless you...
Way down in there

...

...I'm touching your face

...

...

Listen
Listen to me
Don't wake up
Don't bother
Don't bother trying to...*flinch*
Hmhm
Just talk to me
Well
I mean
Feel me...
I'm laying right along the length of you,
I'm a draft excluder
I haven't even taken my shoes off
The silver
You told me you liked them

...

I believed you
My shoes are on the bed
And my skirt
Unpleated...And I'm pulling it...
Up
Up
Above my knees now

...

And if I got up on top of you right now?
Would you...?
And then you'd...
... Hold...
Or...
Just stay there
Hm
Lay there...

...

You've done it before
It's not so different

...

The stars aren't so far away are they?
You remember
Things might be like this forever
You remember the giant picture

I know it
I know it
I'm doing it
I'm right here
You can't take yourself
Haha
I'm on top of you
Freedom is just a cliché
(*Serious.*) Your hands are dry
And I know you
Because I'll be here
More than yesterday
I can see you so clearly now
Have you ever stopped moving?
Hm
I don't recognise you
I don't like you...anymore
Hm
Anymore than before haha
We're neutral
Like me
(*Whispers.*) I'm joking
(*Running fingers through his hair.*) One big lump
Isn't it
Would be nice to see them all in a line
Shining
It's an honest angle
In the soup
You remember
You almost lost a rib
Oh
I pulled mine out so elegantly
From the mouth
It's a stone or a grain of sand
It doesn't mean anything
Hair
You waste everything
But you're getting quieter
The room is talking
Shall I make myself perfectly clear?
All day I'm stopping
It's easy
My company

When I'm carrying
Myself
Along
With me
The bump
And they're...broadcasting
At dawn, the phantom
I was unstuffed
In the morning
Stuffed
Sickly horse
What must everyone think about me?
A surrogate, at the party
Has anyone noticed?
You look kind of deflated
Angel
Queen of women
I'm not conceited
I'm tired
I'm very realistic
I'm a realist
I know what's going to happen
I remember everything
My boy
I'm only joking
I don't feel safe
I am safe
 (Hangs up.)

 End Of Play

Characters:

Voice.   Her mind is caught in two places—both these places are somehow apart from the place where she actually *is*, which might be an office, though we'll never know. She can hear her audience, but she finds it hard to listen to them. She often hangs up when discovering that she has been put on speakerphone. She doesnt want an audience, she is trying to speak to someone.

When developing this project with the actor Valerie McCann, she would dart around the text when confronted by her audience at the other end of the phone, cutting it up at will, inserting lines into their ears, at times blasé, at times threatening. She did this all of her own accord, I just picked up snippets here and there when I could, it was thrilling and felt true to the character and the text.

Author's Notes:

—   This at the start of a sentence indicates speed and urgency.
...   This at the start or end of a sentence indicates a trailing in or off of a sentence, some distance

(Nervously and cautiously at first, but always obnoxious, perhaps drunk.)

H-hello?
Are you there?
...
I'm calling from...*uhh*...from social services
You've been put on a list! Haha
Can you hear me?
Helloooo
...
(Sigh.) Ahaaa another prank call—
No!
I mustn't jump to conclusions!
That's not my job!
I don't have a job! Haha
God people will say anything—
—Look—I'll just say the spiel now in case you really are in a sort of
nightmare

(Big breath in and out.)

Ok!
Woo!
Here we go!
Listen up!
It's my job to say this to you babe, I'm very good at it.
I'm telling you, five-star quality.
Just because I was fired—you know, I mean, don't let that detract from the life I've built here.
12 years in a call centre—
—Well in social services so I got my steps in—you know, servicing the social
I haven't always been *here*—
—It doesn't matter.
Is it believable that I would care?
Am I believable?
Oh I'm just a voice on a phone to you.
Haha I see, yes, if the phone rings, answer it!
If you need help, call!
Wait, ok I haven't even asked you yet!
Well it's not a question just, you know, giving up a baby.
Giving up! Haha

Oh god you do want to give up your baby don't you?
You haven't got the wrong number?
—Oh but that's a thing of the past surely?...
...Darling are you alright?!
Look I'm here to help haha
Believe it or not, I mean we've got better things to do haven't we?
Haha *'we'*.
Me.
God people will say anything—
People will *believe anything*—
And your baby haha!
Bad girl! Haha
My manager will be back any minute so enjoy the show doll—
Men cheat!
Women love! Haha
Don't listen to me haha
The only thing worse than a man is pretty fucking obvious to me.
Aha! Ok! Advice! It's all coming out now—
Things got a lot easier for me when I accepted that women would never respect me.
...
Babe...
...You got kids?

(Quietly laughing—for a bit too long.)

Hahahaha I mean other kids
Ones you're keeping?
Or ones you kept?
It's never too late hun haha—
And they're not yours.
Not really.
They've got you cornered.
I won't lie.
And listen to the way we talk!
It's like men all shrivel up and die

(Big sigh but with a strange bodily sound.)

The TV's on—
My computer—
I'm watching TV
Those boys—

What's your name again?
The way these people talk—
What do I want to say?
What should children see?
I'm talking and I'm watching.
And they're ugly too.
And gorgeous—
You know, how old is this kid?
His fucking tits—
He's crying now—
The other one—
On his dad's shoulder.
Music.
But those tits, haha I'm waking up from a dream!
Those tits!
And they're dressed by adults.
What are they wearing?!
Everything about them their whole world is is...
Ersatz...
—Cocks—I'm not mental, I have eyes.
I've been to foreign countries.
I have people who ask me
(Whining.) Is everything ok? Are you lonely?
I've said it all too.
I've seen a cock become a cunt—hun! I have something!
I'm doing it.
My face is getting hotter and colder.
My eyes are stinging.
Stripped
Drunk
She is drunk
Again,
stripped
Has been
drunk
before,
unstripped
has been
prosecuted
before,
Jury
Has been
caught

Dancing
For me
the slurring
She is
slurring
Long time ago now
Last month
Last
Brown hair
Last black hair
Long and
White!
Female!
She is
She says
are you
Going
And
And to
tase me?
What was that drunk
-Title -
Drunk
drink
I've become... empty, you know.
Because I trust myself.
I will do whatever I tell myself to do.
I will keep hurting myself.
I will reject people over and over, as they do me.
Because I won't stop until I get what I want.
He's shorter than him, you know.
He's arching his feet.
The cock slides right in there and and
women are not allowed here.
...Their hair is crucial and
...
You know...
honestly,
You know I believe in sex

(Pause.)

...
Hi!

Hiii‼...

...

Fucking hell...
It's better isn't it.
To just watch it.
And listen.
This is better.
I'm not everyone.
I don't care anymore.
(Suddenly yelling.) I ONLY CARE ABOUT MY LIFE!

...

My own life

...

...This 14-year-old wants to be a father haha
In New York homeless men masturbate in the street.
Oh all I have is sex now
Is that sad?
It's free.
Until it's not haha! *(Pained coughs.)*
Babe speak to me!
Sex is free!
I've been through a lot but this really is shit.
I've never been you!
I have always longed for the friendship of women!

...

(Hangs up phone.)

End Of Play

Characters:

VOICE.   He focuses and dissociates. He concentrates on a feeling while his words walk ahead of him. He's been drinking. He loses himself in his own volume with crescendos travelling between distant and sensual to an alienated, sharp bellow. He is his volume.

A GOOD FRIEND.   All her friends are women.

Author's Notes:

—   This at the start of a sentence indicates speed and urgency.

A Good Friend.   Hi, stop what you're doing.
He's on stage right now.
How the fuck did he get in here?
(*Indignantly.*) And of course Nobody stopped him.
What the fuck is he doing haha?
Sorry—it's not funny—but *grunts*
If you could see this right now...
He's just stood there!
(*Gleeful.*) Ellie's yelling *'Get off! Get off!'* Hahaha
(*Dread.*) Oh my God he's got the microphone
Oh my God he's talking
Listen

(A Good Friend *holds out her phone in the hope that the person on the other end of the receiver will hear the man on stage.*)

Voice.   (*Speaking into a microphone.*)...
Hm hm dead air, dead air hmm
/Who's even here?
No! don't answer all at once!
And do you remember a boy?
Haha no not that!
Pervert!
Pervert Mr Richards!
Did anyone ever lock that sicko up?

A Good Friend.   Did you hear that?
God there's a lot of people here
(*To someone beside her.*) GET HIM OFF!
...
Fuck.
I don't know what to do.
Listen.

(A Good Friend *holds out her phone again.*)

Voice.   The money's gone from the economy, you know, it's not coming back! Haha

...

'Hey look he was your friend or you didn't have any friends
You remember him.

From before, no nice way of—can't get the rhythm somehow, someone
just told me you know...weeks ago.
Someone just told me.
He grew up, the toddler, never saw him—and if you did you don't
remember—didn't know that was him—really nearby–probably did see...
...
I won't say it.
I think it was Ritherdon Road even, so really—unalived
Stepping in front of, of a—I won't—21 is—and they had a chiiiiild
proooofff gattte...'

(Sniffs or coughs then hangs his head like it's heavy.)
...
Hm hm dead air

A GOOD FRIEND.   /*(Sighing.)* Babe, it's Eric he's on about right?
Did you end up calling his mum?
I mean I know it's awkward....
And where are you by the way?
...*(Sigh.)* I mean I feel like I have to say, you know, I mean...what were you
thinking haha?
He's still up there babe, do you want to just listen to it all?
Oh Catherine's mouthing Turin at me, you're in Turin?
You never tell me anything.
Is that the mountains?
...*(Exhaling.)* You should just listen you know it's none of my business and
I never could stand him but you owe him that much Alison really.
We as, as people. We owe each other so much.
...
I'm holding out my phone again now.

VOICE.   *(In a mocking voice.)* Thank you! Before I heard that I thought
my son was gonna go to hell, but now I *know* he's gonna go to heaven haha!

...

Hm hm dead air.
I think in the olden days, everyone just knew each other.

...

And mad men just wandered through dirt roads, same as now.

...

Ireland *is* full of them haha!

...

It happened a lot at my last school...yeah it's not true you know.
...teacherrrrs and studentsssss, It's not true.
Women allllways do it, they're just bad at it.

...

(Emerging from somewhere deep in thought, whispering.) And I will,
I will sing.

PIECE OF SHIT PARTY!

(Whining, somewhat earnestly.)

Everyone was singing.
She's not dead!

...
...Yeah I could never be myself around Alison...
...I wrote....

(Indignantly.)

All the time! Yeah, I was writing.

(He starts to sing quickly, an unknown flat tune.)

Haha

*(He sings the following lines to a strange tune that doesn't fit the
lyrics, he's made up his own song or he's singing to the tune of a pop
song he heard on the radio.)*

When I walk down the street and I see someone beautiful,
I say hey beautiful!

When I walk down the street and I see someone ugly,
I say hey! Ugly!

(Sings a little more, wordlessly humming.)

Hmm hmmmm hmm hmmmmmmmmm hm hmm hmmmmmmmmmmmm

(Drops microphone on the ground.)

A GOOD FRIEND.   Did you hear all that?
Your dad's just sitting in a corner.
Guinessed.
He looks ...miserable.
I'm sorry hun do you think I should call someone?
—Wait—He's coming towards me—*fuck.*

(The sound of scuffles as VOICE *takes* A GOOD FRIEND'S *phone.)*

VOICE.   *(Gleeful, disturbed, he's got what he wanted.)* Helloooooooooooooo?
Is it you?
It is you!
Whatttt am I too old for you?
We know where you live miss!
Can you give me a gold star?
(Softly) It's better
We're better, like this.
You can hear me!
It's not so bad is it?
Does it snow in Italy, Alison?
Alison!
We are being called for dinner!
Alison what is romance?
What's his body like?
Alison.
He lives in the 8os, he'll die there, he has a marble spiral.
...I remember everything, Alison.
...Does it snow in Italy?

(Suddenly —)

LET ME MAKE MYSELF PERFECTLY CLEAR, BEFORE YOU
TOUCH MY CHILDREN UNDERSTAND THAT I WOULD GO TO
PRISON WITH A SSMILE ON MY FACE FOOR THEM.
YOUR LIFE IS NOTHING TO ME.
MY OWN LIFE IS NOTHING TO ME.

WHEN MY KIDS ARE INVOLVED IT'S—

(Voice *is tackled to the ground. The phone hangs up.*)

End Of Play

Characters:

MAY.   A passive, accommodating voice is here. Available for her audience,
Ambivalently, and more. She is kindly resigned to life (kind to others but
also to herself). She *plays* dumb. She helps people unenthusiastically but
not without force. Present *and* vacant, is she dissociating? Am I? It's very
effective. It's a very efficient performance.

Her voice rings, unanxiously—like tuning forks or a meditation bowl.

Author's Notes:

()   Indicates a pause for the audience's response.

MAY.   Hello

...

I have some questions for you

...

If you're ready, I'll begin?

( )

So

Do you still talk to your family ?

( )

Mhm

( )

Not everyone does

( )

And do you miss them?

( )

Right

Well I am listening, you see?

And I'd like you to say something out loud if you can

In case you're wondering, my name is May

You could speak loudly

So everyone could hear you

Is anyone there with you?

( )

Who?

( )

Is that ok?

( )

Ok well

Either way, here we go

...

Repeat after me

Around the book

( )

It's empty

( )

Like me

( )

When the red light comes on

( )

A real bell moves

( )

And rings

( )

In front

( )

Of the TV

( )

Apparently one of my grenades had connected

( )

I didn't feel anything

( )

I could feel something

( )

Acquiring all those women

( )

I loved it

( )

I lit up the entire valley

( )

Something different every day

( )

Something donuts

( )

I'm gonna be there

( )

I'm going to be there

( )

And so will I

( )

In the new state

( )

The adulthood of humanity.

( )

I always

( )

Always

( )

Forget

( )

That Jesus died at Christmas

( )

We played football

( )

In the snow

( )

I was a boy then

()
It was wonderful
()
(With some quiet urgency)
Kiss me my boy
()
For we'll never movie again
()
We don't all feel the same
()
But I do
()

Eɴᴅ Oꜰ Pʟᴀʏ

Thank you to Valerie McCann, Martin Edwards, Joey Robinson, Biz Lyon, Charlie Mitchell, Markus Bernhard Börger and Lisa Heinrici, who generously collaborated with me on their roles during read throughs and performances, greatly informing the texts.

Scores. 1
Sam Cottington. Phone Plays
ISBN. 978-3-945247-32-7

Editor: Hasti
Second Editor: Emily Pope
Graphic Design: JMMP – Julian Mader, Max Prediger
Print: Memminger MedienCentrum
Edition: 500

Montez Press Ltd.
Unit 29, Penarth Centre
Penarth Street
SE15 1TR, London
United Kingdom

Scores is co-produced by Montez Press
and London Performance Studios.

www.montezpress.com
www.londonperformancestudios.com

m LPS